20
IMAGES
18
SONNETS

Design by Ian G. Rohan
Photography by John G. Stevens

ISBN 978-1-7349263-0-9 (paperback)
ISBN 978-1-7349263-1-6 (ebook)

First edition: May 2020

www.jgstevens.com
www.ianrohanmedia.com

THIS LITTLE BOOK IS DEDICATED TO MY AMAZING DAUGHTER, ORIANA. YOU WILL LEARN A LITTLE BIT ABOUT HER INSIDE, THOUGH A SONNET DID NOT PERMIT ME TO SAY NEARLY ENOUGH ABOUT HER GOOD QUALITIES AND A HAIKU WOULD HAVE BEEN ENTIRELY INSUFFICIENT.

MOST OF THESE PHOTOS WERE TAKEN ON OUR YEARLY JAUNTS TO A NATIONAL PARK (ONE OF ORIANA'S CHRISTMAS PRESENTS), **MANY OF THEM ON A RECENT TRIP TO UTAH'S CANYONLANDS AND ARCHES.**

I TOOK MOST OF THEM WITH A CANON POWERSHOT SX 60 HS. A FEW OF THEM WERE TAKEN WITH MY NEW CANON 5D.

ENJOY!

SONNET I

WE GLIMPSED THE POND AND KNEW WE HAD TO STOP
TO FIND REFLECTIONS OF THAT RICH SANDSTONE
AND THERE WAS COBALT, HEAVEN'S OWN RAINDROP
AN OUTCOME WE COULD NEVER ONCE BEMOAN

LIKE WONDERLAND'S TRANSMUTING LOOKING GLASS
THE WATER'S SURFACE TRANSLATES ALL BENEATH
INTO A PLACE WHERE ANGELS COULD AMASS
THOSE FISSURES BECOME ANGRY OGRE TEETH

THAT ORANGE BUTTE BELOW THE AZURE SKIES
IS FAIR ENOUGH TO LIFT A TROUBLED SOUL
ITS REPRODUCTION EVEN AMPLIFIES
AND ELEVATES THIS POWER TO CONSOLE

THIS MIRROR OUTSIDE UTAH'S CANYONLANDS
TAKES AN EXQUISITE IMAGE AND EXPANDS

SONNET II

WE FAWNED THESE DEAR CRITTERS WITH 'DORING LOOKS
AND STILL THEY SCORNED OUR FRIENDLY OVERTURES
LIKE WE WERE OUTLAWS, LOW-DOWN DIRTY CROOKS
OR CRASS SALESPERSONS WITH NOISOME BROCHURES

ENCOUNTERED NEAR THE TOP OF CUESTA GRADE
THEY BOUNDED UP THE HILLSIDE AFTER MOM
BUT SEPARATED, THEY WERE SORE AFRAID
AND OUR EFFORTS DID NOTHING TO BECALM

THEIR PLAINTIVE CRIES FOR HER TROUBLED OUR HEARTS
AND BROUGHT PRAYERS FOR A SPEEDY REUNION
WITH PROTECTION AS WITH THE BEST RAMPARTS
UNTIL THEY COULD RE'STABLISH COMMUNION

A DELIGHTFUL SURPRISE ON A LONG HIKE
DESPITE THEIR DISCOMFORT IT WAS DREAMLIKE

SONNET III

IT FASCINATES AND COMMANDS SCRUTINY
THIS RARE BOULDER OF ENTRADA SANDSTONE
AGAINST THE DULL MAINSTREAM IN MUTINY
PERCHED HIGH ON A PEDESTAL OF MUDSTONE

EROSION IS THIS MARVEL'S PARENTAGE
HARSH WINTER, SLEET, AND FREEZINGS GAVE HIM SHAPE
WHERE DECLINE, AGING ARE A SACRILEGE
THIS, THE SALIENT FEATURE OF ITS LANDSCAPE

BEAUTY SHORT-LIVED IS WORSHIPED ON THE EARTH
AND THIS BALANCED ROCK STANDS IN STARK CONTRAST
AN AGING PROCESS UNDERLIES ITS WORTH
A PROGRESSION LEAVING YOUTH CULTURE AGHAST

WITH A SHORT HIKE, MISS WORLD STANDS AT ITS BASE
IT TOWERS HIGH ABOVE HER LOVELY FACE

(38 METERS TO BE EXACT)

11

SONNET IV

TWO CROWS SNUGGLE ON ISLAND IN THE SKY
WE FOUND THEM FLYING O'ER THE CANYONLANDS
THEIR HOME FAR MORE MAJESTIC THAN VERSAILLES
SANS LOUIS' GASCONADE OR FALSE COMMANDS

THEY SOARED ABOVE THE MAZE AT GRAND VIEW POINT
AS NONCHALANT AS IF IT WERE A SWAMP
THEN STOOD UPON A PIÑON TREE CONJOINT
IN SIMPLE BONHOMIE SANS ANY POMP

AS TOURISTS MARVELED AT THE SIGHTS BEYOND
THEY DISPLAYED THEIR PREF'RENCE FOR AN EMBRACE
FOR WHICH IT SEEMED THEY NEVER WOULD ABSCOND
THIS MEMORY WE TOO WILL NOT EFFACE

THE WONDERS OF THESE SHEER SANDSTONE CLIFFS HERE
ARE RIVALED BY THIS LOVE STORY SO DEAR

14

SONNET V

THIS WINDOW TO BUCK CANYON AND LA SAL
ILLUMINED BY THE FIRST RAYS OF THE DAWN
ONE ALMOST HEARS AN ANGELIC CHORALE
AND ENVISIONS RICH CULTURES LONG BYGONE

ORIANA VIEWED THIS ORIANA
FULLY ENGROSSED, STANDING AT THE CLIFF'S EDGE
IN HER MIND SURELY ROSE AN HOSANNA
HER GRATEFUL HEART INVIGORATES HER PLEDGE

SPARKLES GOLD AND PINK SHOWED IN THE CANYONS
JUST AHEAD OF THE SUN'S LEADING SALUTES
DETACHED IN TIME, THEY'RE STILL CLOSE COMPANIONS
TO ASTONISH US THEY ARE IN CAHOOTS

SO ICONIC THIS VIEW FROM MESA ARCH
THE COLD DROVE US AWAY IN A QUICK MARCH

16

SONNET VI

ANSEL MADE KNOWN THIS IMAGE TO THE WORLD
SIMILAR CLOUDS THREATENED IN THIRTY-FOUR
BUT THEN THE BRIDE'S VEIL STEADILY WHIRLED
WAS CAPTURED FAR BETTER BY MY MENTOR

HOW MANY TIMES HAVE STORMS ASSAILED THIS SCENE?
BROUGHT FLOODS CALAMITOUS, STONE-BREAKING COLD?
YET HAVE NOT CHASED GLAMOUR FROM THIS RAVINE
NOR DIMINISHED ONE BIT WHAT WE BEHOLD

STILL I COWER WITH EACH APPROACHING SQUALL
FORGETFUL OF THE ONE WHO PRESERVES LIFE
WHO MAY PERMIT ROUGH WINDS ACROSS NIGHTFALL
ONLY TO BIRTH NEW GEMS AS A MIDWIFE

IF GOD SAFEGUARDS THIS TUNNEL VIEW FROM LOSS
MUCH MORE AM I PROTECTED BY HIS CROSS

SONNET VII

JABBA THE HUTT, AN UNASHAMED OUTLAW
HE WAS A MURDERER, A VILE WRETCH
BUT HIS COUSINS WERE PURE WITH NO SUCH FLAW
MARVELOUS ARTISTS WHO COULD WEAVE AND SKETCH

TO THE AMERICAN SOUTHWEST THEY MOVED
UNCOMMON LANDSCAPES THERE INSPIRED THEIR CRAFT
AND IN THE DRY CLIMATE THEIR HEALTH IMPROVED
THEY EVEN DABBLED IN UTAH STATECRAFT

THEY LIKE TO SIT AND WATCH THE LA SAL RANGE
WITH SANDSTONE MESAS LOOMING IN THE FORE
ADMITTEDLY THEY APPEAR RATHER STRANGE
THEIR CREATIVE JUICES ROUSED TO A POUR

THE NAME OF HUTT WAS BESMEARED BY A CAD
THEIR UTAH REPUTATION'S NOT SO BAD

SONNET VIII

BEFORE CLIMBING TO THAT GLACIER'S PEAK
WE AMBLED THROUGH SUCH MEADOWS, GREEN AND COOL
STOPPING TO HEAR SOME MUSIC FROM THIS CREEK
COULD THERE BE A MORE TRANSCENDENT HIKE-FUEL?

THE WALK BESIDE THE WATER, EFFORTLESS
NOT SO THE TREK TO CONQUER MT. LASSEN
THE ASCENT STEEP, OUR FOOTHOLDS DUBIOUS
THE SLIPP'RY ICE COULD BE OUR ASSASSIN

YET SHASTA'S DAZZLING VIEW FROM THE APEX
UTTERLY JUSTIFIED ADVERSITY
ONE DOES NOT THINK OF TROUBLES DURING SEX
TO DO SO WOULD BE A GREAT PERVERSITY

PEACEFUL MEANDERING IS SO SUBLIME
AND STRUGGLE-FED JOYS CAP THOSE OF PEACETIME

SONNET IX

"PASS THROUGH THIS PORTAL TO A WONDERLAND,"
DECREES THIS RAVEN MOST COMPELLINGLY
"YOUR DAYS THERE NEVER MUNDANE NOR QUITE BLAND"
THE RICHES THERE HE DESCRIBES TELLINGLY:

"THE SNOW BEYOND THIS ARCH WARMS HUMAN FLESH
THE AIR ATOP THAT RANGE WILL MELT YOUR YEARS
HOPE IS REKINDLED THERE AS BY A CRECHE
THE SWEETEST MUSIC ENTERS IN BOTH EARS

"EV'RY CHILD THERE RECEIVES HUGS ALL DAY LONG
AND LIMA BEANS ARE BARRED AT THE BORDER
YOU PAY FOR YOUR GROCERIES WITH A SONG
THERE IS NO CORPORATE CRIME, NO RANK HOARDER

"ENTER!" HE SPOKE, "BUT LEAVE YOUR CELL PHONE HERE."
HIS LISTENER DEPARTS LEAVING BUT A TEAR

23

SONNET X

THE CHEERFUL HEAD OF A MALE HOUSE FINCH
APPEARED IN OUR KITCHEN GARDEN TODAY
AND WHEN I WALKED OUTSIDE HE DID NOT FLINCH
OR SHOW AFFRIGHT AND SWIFTLY FLY AWAY

HE CASUALLY RECOMMENCED HIS MEAL
OF OLD SUNFLOWER SEEDS UPON THOSE STALKS
BLISSFULLY UNAWARE OF HIS APPEAL
HE DINED AMID CINDY AND JOANIE'S TALKS

HIS HEART'NING VISIT HAD NOT BEEN FORECAST
AT BREAKFAST WE DID NOT KNOW OF THIS PRIZE
YET WE STILL RECALL OF HIS QUIET REPAST
AND CELEBRATE UNEXPECTED ALLIES

A VISIT LONG-ENSHRINED IN OUR MEM'RY
PROFOUND AND YET SO ELEMENTARY

SONNET XI

SETTING INDELIBLY ON CANYON WALLS
THE SUN LIT THIS WIDE CANVAS FULL ABLAZE
IN SIMPLIFYING OUR TASK OF RECALLS
IT ENSURED WE'D REC'LLECT THIS NIGHT ALWAYS

OCHRE AND CADMIUM PIGMENTS HE USED
TO FAR SURPASS THE GENIUS OF MONET
HAVING THE SAME IMPRESSION, NOT ABUSED
CLAUDE WOULD BOW TO THE CLOSING OF THIS DAY

JUST MOMENTS HENCE THE MURAL IS ERASED
THE GRAND COLORS REMOVED AND SET AWAY
BY MOON SHADOWS AND DIMNESS THEN REPLACED
WITHOUT A SCUFFLE OR A GRIM AFFRAY

THE SUN'S ARTISTRY WAS ON FULL DISPLAY
HIS CRAFT AND EXPERTISE WE'LL NOT DOWNPLAY

SONNET XII

THE DAY'S FINAL RAYS FELL UPON THIS STONE
AS OUR TIME IN ARCHES CAME TO A CLOSE
I GRABBED MY CAM'RA AND COULD NOT POSTPONE
LEST THE IMAGE BE NOTHING BUT SHADOWS

SHARPLY DIVIDING HIGHLIGHTS FROM THE SHADE
A LINE DISSECTS IT BOTTOM FROM ITS TOP
THE QUINTESSENCE OF CONTRAST THUS DISPLAYED
LIKE A KARDASHIAN IN A GRIM SWEATSHOP

THE LA SAL RANGE IS SNOW-CAPPED JUST BEYOND
AND CLOUDS ADORN THE SKY AS DARKNESS SPREADS
REVEALING JEWELS, THE LIGHT NOW DOES ABSCOND
SWIFTLY DISPATCHED LIKE LOVERS TO THEIR BEDS

DAZZLING REMEMBRANCES HAVE FILLED THIS DAY
AND YET ONE LAST AS SUNSHINE DOES GIVE WAY

30

SONNET XIII

A TURQUOISE WAVE BREAKS ON THE PEBBLY SHORE
HIGH ABOVE A SUMPTUOUS GARDEN BECKONS
MY LOVE AND I SAT THERE TO EACH EXPLORE
THE JOLTING HARDSHIPS ONE NEVER RECKONS

THE BRILLIANT COLORS AND THE DOLPHIN'S CRY
EACH SOFTEN THE STING OF RECENT SORROW
ABATE A GRIEF WE CANNOT SATISFY
ALL THIS BEAUTY FOR A DAY WE BORROW

FURTHER NORTH WE'LL WALK IN SHADING REDWOODS
TO DEEPEN AND ENHANCE THE HEALING WORK
AT NEPENTHES, SOME TEA AND CHOICE BAKED GOODS
IN CONCERT WILL DISPERSE OUR POOR SOULS' MURK

WE SIT NOT PASSIVELY WHEN DISTRESS MOUNTS
BUT FLY TO BEAUTIES OF IMMENSE ACCOUNT

FOREVER DRAWN

WHO IS THIS COURAGEOUS YOUNG WOMAN
HIKING INTO ANY LANDSCAPE
NO MATTER HOW HARD OR SINGULARLY ODD?

SHE HAS BEEN TO THE TOP OF WHITNEY
SHE SEEMED TO FLY TO THE TOP OF LASSEN
WHILE I FOLLOWED FAR BEHIND
WITH MY "CAUTIOUS OLD LADY STEPS"

I REMEMBER WHEN SHE WAS AFRAID TO ASK THE TIME OF DAY
FROM A DESK CLERK AT THE AHWAHNEE
OR LOOK A VISITOR IN THE EYE

HOW THINGS HAVE CHANGED!

NOW SHE GOES TO FOREIGN LANDS TO MINISTER TO ABUSED WOMEN
SHE DELIVERS NEWBORNS IN POVERTY-WRACKED COMPOUNDS
FAR FROM THE AID OF PROPER MEDICAL CARE

NOW SHE GOES WHERE HER LORD REQUIRES

SHE MAY NOT BE ENTIRELY CLEAR ABOUT HER MARCHING ASSIGNMENT
BUT SHE TRUSTS HIS GUIDANCE AND PROTECTION
SO SHE MOVES FORWARD

SHE IS FOREVER IN SEARCH OF BEAUTY
FOREVER DRAWN BY THE CHALLENGE
OF EXPERIENCING NATURAL BEAUTIES FIRSTHAND
IN WILD LOCATIONS THAT DETER THE FAINT OF HEART

**FOREVER COMMITTED TO EXTENDING
HER LORD'S HEALING POWER TO OTHERS**

I AM IN AWE OF THIS CHANGE

I AM IN AWE OF THIS COURAGEOUS YOUNG WOMAN

33

STARLING MURMURS

A STARLING MURMURS
FAR UP IN SHADOWED GREEN'RY
IT IS A HIGH "COO"

SONNET XIV

WITH THESE LUTRINAE I IDENTIFY
THIER LOVE OF PLAY, THEIR PASSION FOR SHELLFISH
AND SNUGGLING WITH ONE'S DEAR FRIENDS SO CLOSE BY
THEY EMBODY MY ULTIMATE LIFE WISH

I WONDER WHY GOD BIRTHED ME ON THE LAND
WHEN A SINGU'RLY GREAT PUP I WOULD MAKE
IF THE PACIFIC WERE MY FATHERLAND
I MAY NOT HAVE ENGENDERED SUCH HEARTACHE

I'D WRAP MY TWINS UP TIGHT IN SOME SEAWEED
AND DIVE TO ABALONE FOR THEIR SNACK
ALL OTHER SELFISH DUTIES I'D CONCEDE
MY MINISTRY TO PROVIDE WHAT THEY LACK

WHEN HUMAN PARENTING SEEMS TOO DAUNTING
MY IMAG'NATION GIVES WHAT I'M WANTING

SONNET XV

THIS BARN AND RANCH BELOW THE TETON RANGE
KINDLED A FLIGHT OF FANCY FOR A SWITCH
MORE EVEN THAN OUR ADDRESS WE'D EXCHANGE
SUCH BEAUTY HAS THE VIRTUE TO BEWITCH

BUT WHAT OF THE GOOD FRIENDS WE LEAVE BEHIND?
DO HUGS HAVE MORE VALUE THAN THIS RICH VIEW?
DO TRANSPARENT DISCUSSIONS UNCONFINED
ECLIPSE OUR NEED FOR MOUNTAIN, STREAM, SKY BLUE?

A MULE DEER CANNOT HOLD ME WHEN I WEEP
WAPATI CANNOT CATCH MY FALLING TEARS
THAT COOL STREAM COULD NOT WARM ME WHILE I SLEEP
THIS GORGEOUS STUFF FALLS SHORT OF OUR GOOD PEERS

THE MAJESTIC GRAND TETON DOES ASTOUND
BUT GREATER STILL, OUR FRIENDSHIPS SO PROFOUND

SONNET XVI

WHIRLING TEA CUPS, VIVIDLY CHROMATIC
DIAPHANOUS LANTERNS HANG UP ABOVE
CHARLES AND I FOUND REST HOME'STATIC
FROM ALL THE DREADFUL LINES WE DID NOT LOVE

PAUSING BEFORE OUR PHOTOS WITH ALICE
WE HOPED TO LIFT THE DORMOUSE'S SPIRITS HIGH
SHIELD HIM FROM THE HATTER'S FURTHER MALICE
HIS SAGGING SELF-CONCEPT TO FORTIFY

BUT ONE CANNOT LIFT WHAT ONE DOES NOT SEE
ABANDONING OUR TASK WE WALKED ALONG
AND HOPED OUR PIT'FUL FRIEND WOULD FIND MERCY
AS WE MADE OUR WAY THROUGH THE SHOVING THRONG

AFTER OUR BRIEF CUP AND SAUCER REPOSE
CHARLES AND FAIR ALICE DID JUXTAPOSE

SONNET XVII

THINK ON THINGS LIKE THIS FLO'ER, DIRECTS SAINT PAUL
LOVELY, EXCELLENT, AND WORTHY OF PRAISE
IT NULLIFIES OUR ENEMY'S CABAL
LIFTING OUR POOR SOULS FROM A DEEP MALAISE

ITS MUSIC, THOUGH SILENT, IS ELEGANT
INSPIRING TEN THOUSAND ANGELS TO DANCE
SIMPLICITY THAT CHIDES THE ARROGANT
BATTLING DISCOURAGEMENT, IT IS A LANCE

REM'NISCENT OF A SAT'NY BRIDAL GOWN
THERE'S PURITY ENWRAPPED IN ITS WARFARE
THIS PRINCESS BRIDE WILL FORCIBLY CAST DOWN
THOSE ENTITIES IN THAT FOUL LEGIONNAIRE

TO PONDER ALL THAT IS ADMIRABLE
WE SELECT FROM THE INNUMERABLE

SONNET XVIII

A STARK CONTRAST OF THUNDER AND FINE MIST
ASTOUNDS A VISITOR TO BURNEY FALLS
VIGOR AND DELICACY COEXIST
AS SUMO WRESTLERS PLAY WITH PORC'LAIN DOLLS

ONE HUNDRED MILLION GALLONS CRASH EACH DAY
UPON A DEEP BLUE POOL WITH MOSSY ROCKS
QUENCHING ONE'S THIRST FOR BEAUTY FULL AWAY
THOUGH SUCH RELIEF IS NOT QUITE ORTHODOX

BLACK SWIFTS HEAR THAT THUNDER AS LULLABIES
NESTLING THEIR YOUNG IN DAMP CAVES ON THE WALL
AT LEAST IT DAMPENS ALL THEIR PRESSING CRIES
PERHAPS PARING MOMS' NEED FOR ALCOHOL?

LIKE SWIFTS I HAVE DIVED INTO THAT COLD MERE
AND WATCHED MY TENSION SWIFTLY DISAPPEAR

45

ABOUT THE AUTHOR & PHOTOGRAPHER

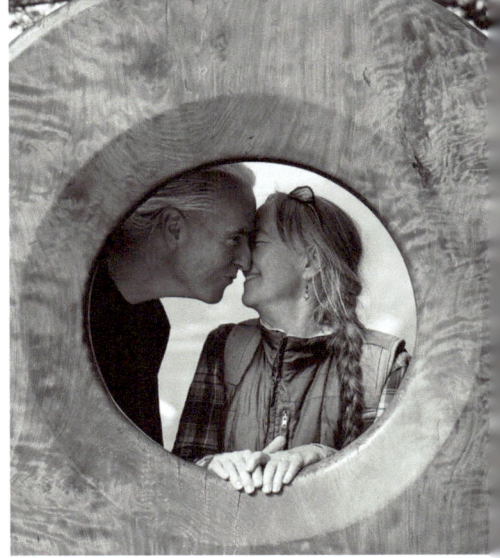

JOHN STEVENS IS A CALIFORNIAN AUTHOR AND PHOTOGRAPHER WITH DEGREES IN BIOCHEMISTRY AND COUNSELING PSYCHOLOGY. HIS FIRST PUBLISHED BOOK, BAJA'S WOUNDED HEALER, DETAILS THE STORY OF A CLOSE FRIEND, DOROTHY, WHO RUNS A HOME FOR TRAFFICKED WOMEN IN BAJA.

JOHN LIVES ON A SMALL GOAT FARM ON CALIFORNIA'S CENTRAL COAST WITH HIS WIFE, CINDY, WHO IS BY FAR THE MORE INTERESTING AND GIFTED OF THE TWO, AND WHO WOULD NEVER BORE YOU WITH SILLY POEMS ABOUT JABBA THE HUTT.

IF YOU WOULD ENJOY BROWSING MORE OF JOHN'S PHOTOGRAPHY, SEARCH FOR JOHN STEVENS AT WWW.500PX.COM: OR IF YOU'D LIKE TO READ MORE OF HIS WRITTEN WORK, VISIT WWW.JGSTEVENS.COM. DON'T WORRY, THE SHORT STORY ABOUT PETER FALK BEING MISTAKEN FOR THE HOLY SPIRIT HAS NOT YET BEEN POSTED.

READ
MORE

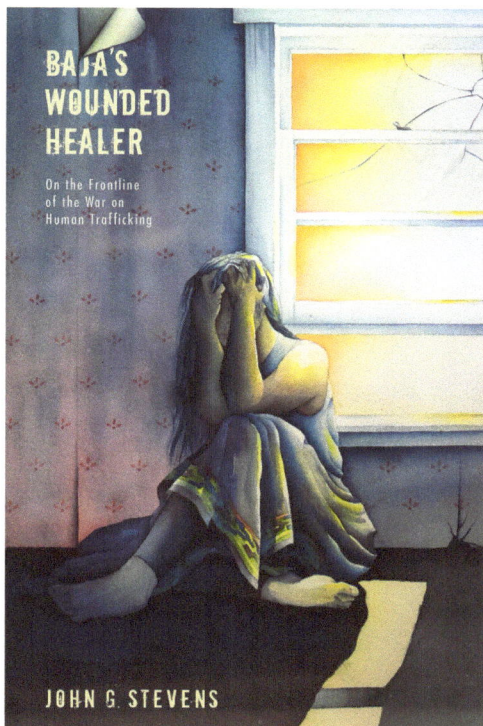

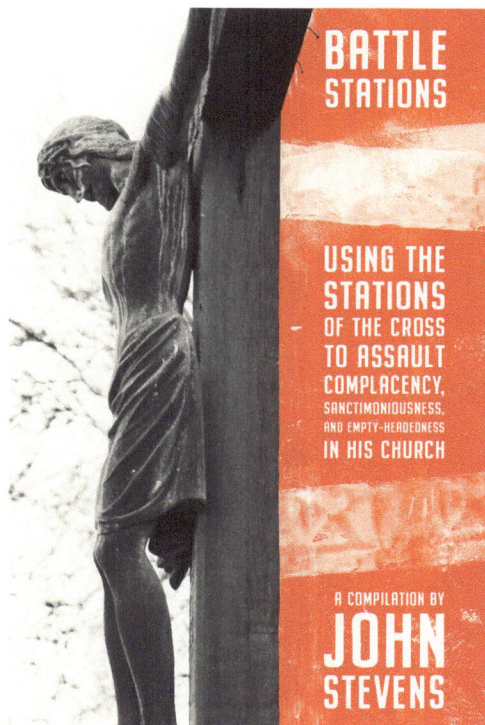

BAJA'S WOUNDED HEALER: ON THE FRONTLINE OF THE WAR ON HUMAN TRAFFICKING IS AN ATTEMPT TO BRING ATTENTION TO ONE SUCCESSFUL BATTLE AGAINST HUMAN TRAFFICKING, AIMING TO INSPIRE MANY IN THE CHRISTIAN CHURCH TO BECOME ENGAGED IN THE FIGHT, AND DEMONSTRATING THE LIBERATING POWER OF GOD'S TRUTH IN COMBATTING ONE OF THE EARTH'S GREAT SCOURGES.

COMING SOON: BATTLE STATIONS: USING THE STATIONS OF THE CROSS TO ASSAULT COMPLACENCY, SANCTIMONIOUSNESS, AND EMPTY-HEADEDNESS IN HIS CHURCH

ABOUT THE DESIGNER

IANROHAN MEDIA

IAN ROHAN IS A CALIFORNIAN ARTIST, GRAPHICS DESIGNER, AND WEB DEVELOPER. HIS PORTFOLIO INCLUDES BRANDING AND ADVERTISING MATERIALS, ALBUM COVERS, BOOKS, WEB DESIGNS, AND MORE, CUSTOM-BUILT FOR A WIDE VARIETY OF BUSINESSES, CREATIVES, AND ORGANIZATIONS. BROWSE HIS WORK AT **WWW.IANROHANMEDIA.COM** OR BY VISITING **IAN ROHAN MEDIA** ON INSTAGRAM.

www.ingramcontent.com/pod-product-compliance
Lightning Source LLC
Chambersburg PA
CBHW041822040426
42448CB00026B/5